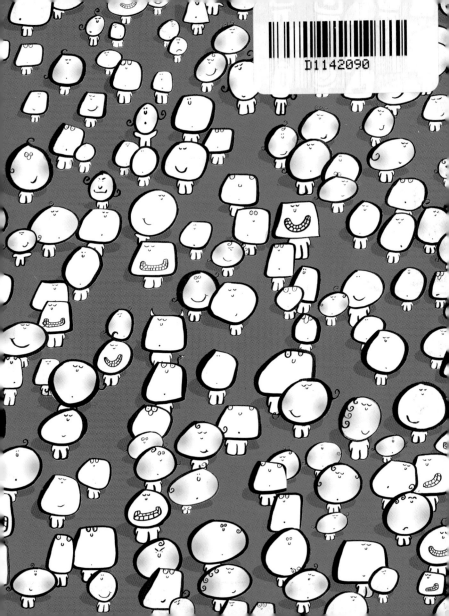

love

with Vimrod

love

You and me...
...two hamsters on the spinning-wheel of **life**

Vimrd by Lisa Swerling and Ralph Lazar

HarperCollins*Publishers*

i wanna hug ya
like da donut hugs
da hole in da donut

in the
lunchbox
of life,

you are the surprise
little yummy
thing that
someone
snuck in.

life is sweet. sweets are sweeter. you are the sweetest.

the last cherry on the cherry tree hopes that **you** will pick it,

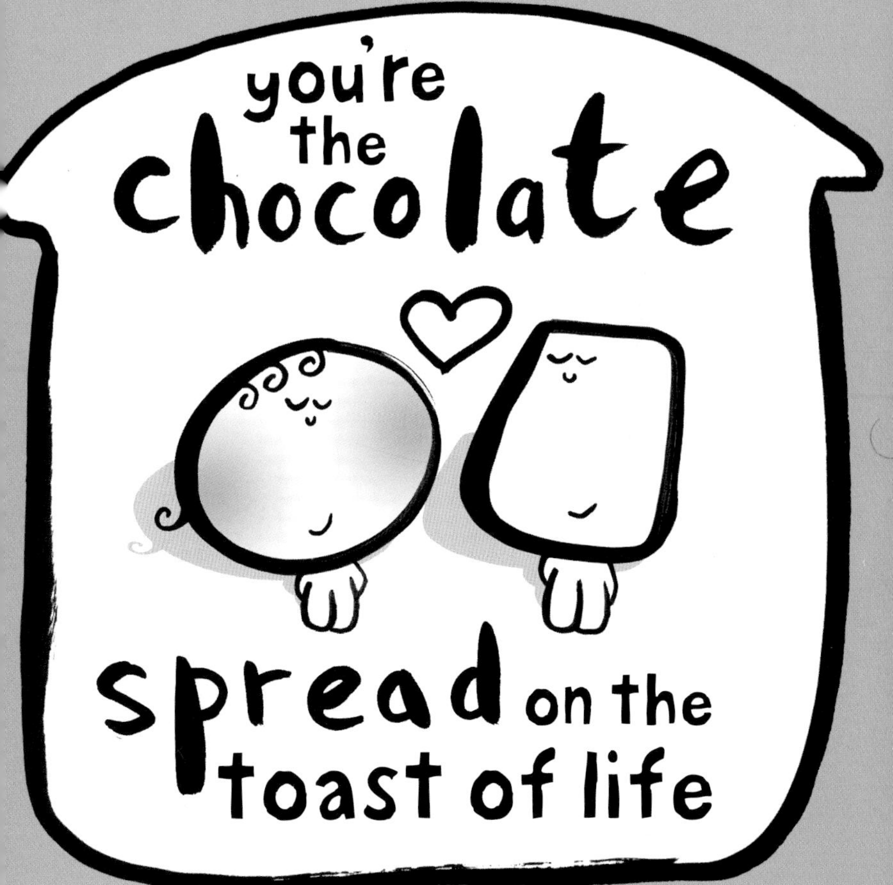
you're the chocolate
spread on the toast of life

how come
you are so

squishy

when you wake up?

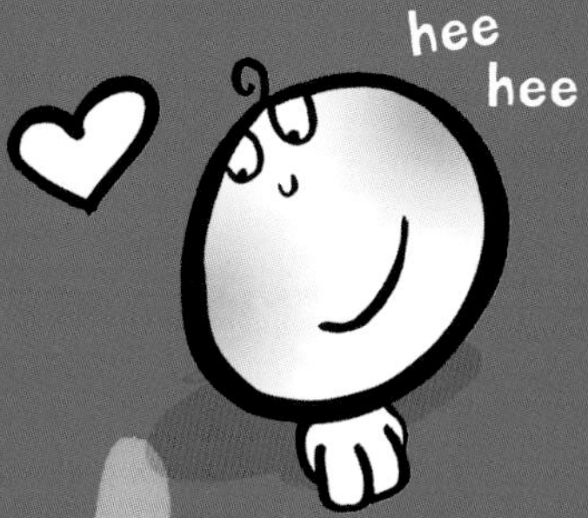

i'll tickle your fancy

if you tickle mine

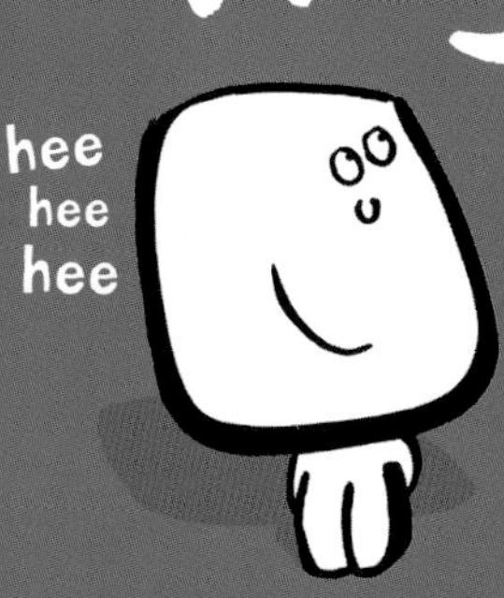

there are only **two**
hands i want to hold:
one is yours, the other
one is your other one.

you tickle my fancy,
swizzle my snizzle,
prickle my shtinkle,
honk on my **stonkle**

and
tingle
my winkle.

YOU

is the meaning of life

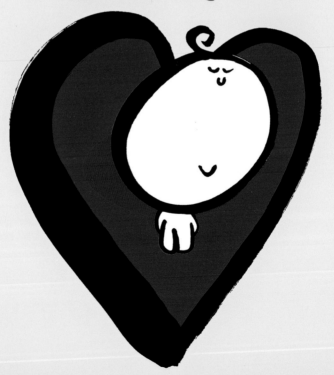

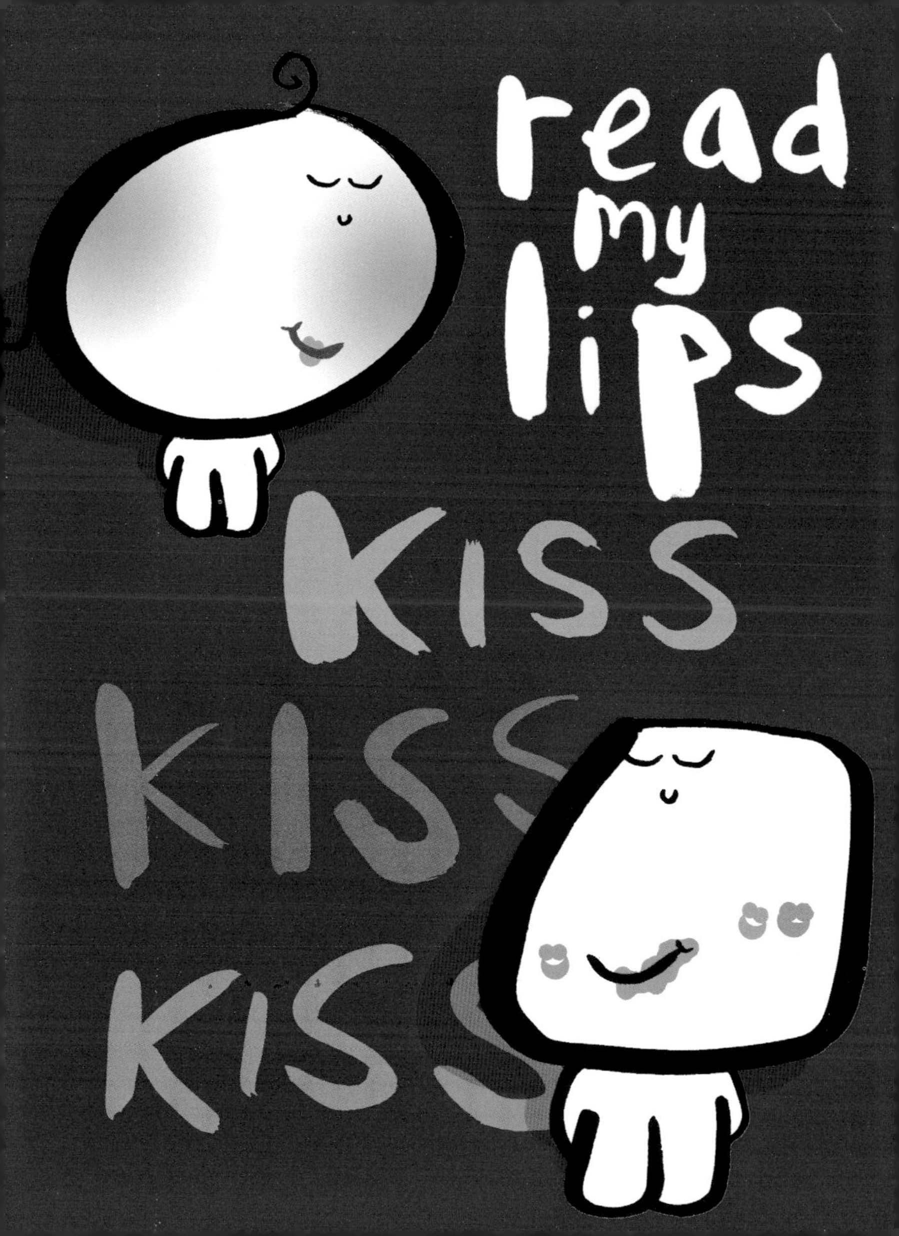
read
my
lips
KISS
KISS
KISS

i love you so much

let's fly
to the moon
and back (we can stop
there for a quick pee,
though, if you need one).

oink oink
be my
mud

you have an

exceptionally

sexy

og-
-gggggggggy-
tokkktokk

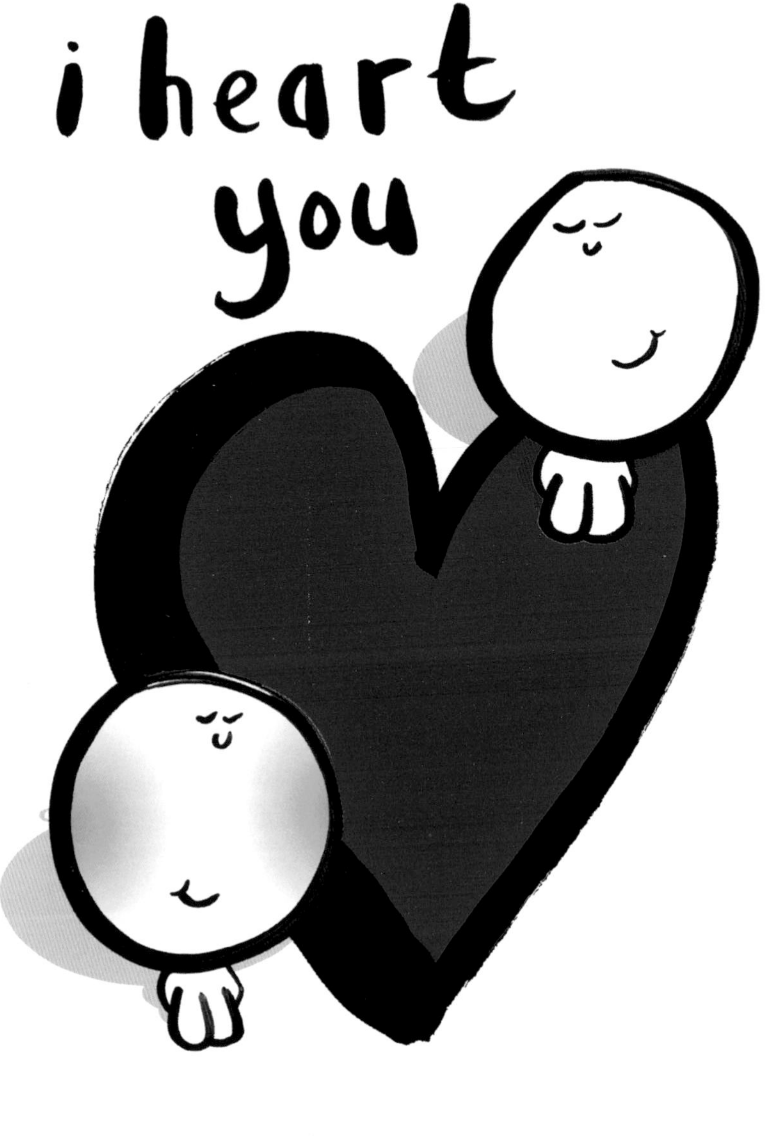
i heart you

are two of the UK's most familiar
graphic artists. Through their company
Last Lemon they have spawned a catwalk
of popular cartoon characters, which
includes Harold's Planet, The Brainwaves,
Blessthischick and, of course, Vimrod.

writers, artists and designers, they are
married with two children, and spend
their time between London and various
beaches on the Indian Ocean.

HarperCollins*Publishers*

77–85 Fulham Palace Road, Hammersmith, London W6 8JB

www.harpercollins.co.uk

Published by HarperCollins*Publishers* 2007

1

A catalogue record for this book is available from the British Library

ISBN-10   0 00 724205 0
ISBN-13   978 0 00 724205 4

Set in Bokka

Printed and bound in Italy by Lego SpA

drink!
Wine is made to be drunk,
I am drunk,
therefore
am I wine?

Vimrod by Lisa Swerling and Ralph Lazar

shopping
it's the little voices that tell me to
go shopping

Vimrod by Lisa Swerling & Ralph Lazar

farting
my farts hospitalise small children

Vimrod by Lisa Swerling & Ralph Lazar

Xmas
christmas is coming run!

Vimrod by ...RLING & RALPH LAZAR

chocolate
life is a struggle between good, evil and chocolate

Vimrod by Lisa Swerling & Ralph Lazar

dads
life is a journey between the fridge and the sofa

Vimrod by Lisa Swerling and Ralph Lazar

mums
behind every great woman is her bum

Vimrod by Lisa Swerling and Ralp...

(watch this space)

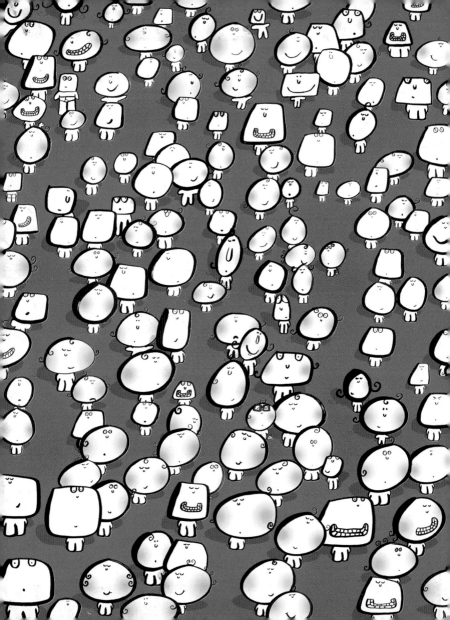